MA)

TIMOTHY TUNNY
SWALLOWED
A BUNNY

BY BILL GROSSMAN
ILLUSTRATED BY KEVIN HAWKES

A   OOK

Library of Congress Cataloging-in-Publication Data
Grossman, Bill.
   Timothy Tunny swallowed a bunny / by Bill Grossman ; illustrated by Kevin Hawkes.
        p.   cm.
   Summary: Presents eighteen whimsical poems about people caught in unusual situations.
   ISBN 0-06-028010-7 – ISBN 0-06-028758-6 (lib. bdg.)
   1. Children's poetry, American.   [1. Nonsense verses.   2. American poetry.]   I. Hawkes, Kevin, ill.   II.
Title.
PS3557.R6715 T56   2000   99-48093
811'.54–dc21   CIP
                                                                                                                        AC

Typography by Alicia Mikles
1 2 3 4 5 6 7 8 9 10
❖
First Edition

To Aunts Marian,
Carol, and Shirley
—BG

To Glen,
a great teacher
—KH

TIMOTHY TUNNY

Timothy Tunny
Swallowed a bunny.
The bunny got lodged in his throat.
"That bunny looks funny,"
His mom said, "but Honey,
Be thankful it isn't a goat."

THE WOMAN IN TOWN

There's a woman in town
Who's afraid that she'll drown
If ever her nose should get wet.
So she wears on her snoot
A small scuba suit.
And it works—she hasn't drowned yet.

HANNIBAL

"Good morning," said Hannibal,
Greeting the cannibal.
"I'm Hannibal. How do you do."

"At the moment you're Hannibal,"
Responded the cannibal,
"But soon we'll be calling you Stew."

THE BARBER

She was cutting his hair,
But he slipped in his chair,
And she lopped off his ears as she cut.
She shouted, "My shears
Have lopped off your ears!"
And he looked up and said to her, "What?"

THE MAN WHO INSISTS THAT HE DOESN'T EXIST

A man who insists

That he doesn't exist

Keeps jumping in puddles of mud.

"I'm glad I'm not here,"

He says, "for I fear

If I were, I'd be covered with crud."

POOR DAD

A witch mean and bad
Imprisoned poor Dad
In a bottle of pop in the closet.
We couldn't free Dad
And were sad when we had
To return him for the nickel deposit.

OLD NED

You're walking, Old Ned,
With a horse on your head.
Why? That can't be much fun.
"I'm *walking*," says Ned,
"With my horse on my head
Because I'm too tired to *run*."

WALTER LACKWARDS

Walter Lackwards,
Head on backwards,
Tripped on things he passed.
He couldn't see
Where next he'd be—
Just where he'd fallen last.

JOHN PAUL MULLERS

John Paul Mullers
Got coated with colors
When some buckets of paint blew apart.
We put John Paul
In a frame on the wall.
Now everyone knows him as "Art."

MR. McFYFE

Mr. McFyfe,
You've sat on your wife
For so long that I'm willing to bet
That you've sat on your wife
For all of her life.
"Nope," says McFyfe. "Not yet."

BILL HACKBAR

In college Bill Hackbar
Worked in the snack bar,
Where pizzas and milkshakes abounded.
He gained little knowledge
From four years in college,
But ended up very well rounded.

JOHN B., ED B., AND LIZ B.

It used to be neat
Playing games in the street
With John B. and Ed B. and Liz B.—
Till we got in the way
Of a dump truck one day.
Now all we're good for is Frisbee.

KEVIN T. MOSES

Kevin T. Moses
Has seventeen noses.
Each birthday he grows a new nose.
What will he do
When he's seventy-two
With all of the noses he grows?

SQUEAKY-CLEAN KEITH

Squeaky-clean Keith
Brushed all his teeth
Every day, every hour, every minute.
Eventually, it's said,
He brushed away his head,
Along with everything in it.

SKINNY YOUNG JANE

Skinny young Jane
Slid down the drain
And flowed through the pipes growing madder.
She said with a shiver
As she entered the river,
"There are times when I wish I were fatter."

JOE TATE

Each supper Joe Tate
Became what he ate—
Be it pork chop or pickle or pear—
Till one supper last fall
He ate nothing at all,
And, *poof*!, he was no longer there.

HAROLD B. BOUND

Harold B. Bound
Turned his eyeballs around
To see all the thoughts in his head.

What do you see
In your head, Harold B.?
"Nothing but cobwebs," he said.

TOM MORSE

"Hey, Mom," says Tom Morse,
Whose mom is a horse,
"May I go to the playground and play?"
His mom tries her best
To tell her son, "Yes,"
But she can't—she can only say "Nay."